HELPFUL PEOPLE
POSTAL WORKER

JAMIE FICKETT

NorwoodHouse Press

Library of Congress Cataloging-in-Publication Data:

Names: Fickett, Jamie.
Title: Postal worker / Jamie Fickett.
Description: Buffalo, NY : Norwood House Press, 2025. | Series: Helpful people | Includes glossary and index.
Identifiers: ISBN 9781684503049 (pbk.) | ISBN 9781684503056 (library bound) | ISBN 9781684503063 (ebook)
Subjects: LCSH: Postal service--Juvenile literature. | Postal service--Employees--Juvenile literature.
Classification: LCC HE6078.F535 2025 | DDC 383--dc23

Published in 2025 by
Norwood House Press
2544 Clinton Street
Buffalo, NY 14224

Designer: Ocean Books
Editor: Kim Thompson

Photo credits: Cover, p. 1 Monkey Business Images/Shutterstock.com; pp. 5, 8, 15 USPS; p. 6 Jillian Cain Photography/Shutterstock.com; p. 7 Ken Wolker/Shutterstock.com; pp. 11, 16 eddtoro/Shutterstock.com; p. 12 Joseph Sohm/Shutterstock.com; p. 13 Olga Popova; p. 17 Indypendenz/Shutterstock.com; p. 19 Brian A Jackson/Shutterstock.com; p. 21 Daniel Afzal/USPS

Printed in the United States of America

CPSIA compliance information: Batch #CW25NHP: For further information contact Norwood House Press at 1-800-237-9932.

TABLE OF CONTENTS

What Is a Postal Worker? 4

What Does a Postal Worker Wear? 10

What Tools Does a Postal Worker Use? 14

How Do You Become a Postal Worker? 18

Glossary 22

Thinking Questions 23

Index 24

About the Author 24

WHAT IS A POSTAL WORKER?

Postal workers are important helpers in our **community**. They deliver mail to homes and businesses. They make sure letters and packages get to the right people.

Postal workers pick up mail that people want to send. They take it to the post office.

Postal workers run the post office. They sell stamps, help people mail packages, and answer questions.

www.us

If a piece of mail is lost, postal workers help find it. If something does not arrive on time, postal workers look for where it might be.

WHAT DOES A POSTAL WORKER WEAR?

The postal worker **uniform** is a shirt and pants in blue or gray colors. The shirt has an eagle **logo** on it.

Postal workers wear comfortable shoes because they walk a lot. Their shoes must keep their feet dry in rain and snow.

Postal workers often wear a hat to protect themselves from the sun. Their hats show the eagle postal service logo.

Some postal workers wear a **waterproof** jacket. It has pockets for holding pens and notepads.

WHAT TOOLS DOES A POSTAL WORKER USE?

Postal workers use **tools** to help them deliver mail **efficiently**. Some carry a mailbag over their shoulder. It holds letters and small packages they need to deliver.

UNITED STATES
POSTAL SERVICE
PRIORITY
MAIL

Postal workers use handcarts and trolleys. They load them up with packages and roll them along.

Postal workers use **scanners** to track packages. They scan each package as it is delivered.

HOW DO YOU BECOME A POSTAL WORKER?

Postal workers must finish high school. They need to be at least 18 years old.

People who want to be postal workers **apply** for a job at the post office. They take a test to see how well they can sort mail.

Good postal workers are organized and careful. They are friendly and helpful. They work hard to make sure everyone's mail gets to the right place.

GLOSSARY

apply (uh-PLYE): to request something officially; to ask for a job

community (kuh-MYOO-ni-tee): a social group of any size whose members live together, have a common government, and often share the same culture or history

efficiently (i-FISH-uhnt-lee): in the best possible way with the least waste of time and effort

logo (LOH-goh): a distinctive symbol or picture that identifies a company or organization

scanners (SKAN-urz): machines that use beams of light to read barcodes and other forms of information

tools (toolz): pieces of equipment that you use to do a job; things that help you reach a goal

uniform (YOO-nuh-form): a special set of clothes worn by all members of a profession, organization, or rank

waterproof (WAW-tur-proof): made of a special material, such as rubber, that does not let water through

THINKING QUESTIONS

1. What is the job of a postal worker?
2. Why does a postal worker wear a hat?
3. How is a postal worker helpful to the community?
4. What are the characteristics of a good postal worker?
5. Would you like to become a postal worker? Why or why not?

INDEX

eagle 10, 12

handcarts 16

lost 9

mailbag 14

post office 6, 7, 19

sort 19

stamps 7

test 19

ABOUT THE AUTHOR

Jamie Fickett lives on Long Island, New York, where he grew up. Every Saturday he enjoys going to the Bronx Zoo and seeing the rhinos from the Wild Asia Monorail. Rhinoceroses have been his favorite animal ever since he was eight and received the nickname Rhino while playing catcher in Little League baseball.